Safari Grammar

a pleasant and educational trip through Grammarland

Written and illustrated by Mario Risso
with a great deal of writing from Marge Truzz
and writing assistance from Nancy Risso.

PASSPORT BOOKS
a division of *NTC Publishing Group*
Lincolnwood, Illinois USA

Also available: Safari Punctuation

1991 Printing

Published by Passport Books, a division of NTC Publishing Group.
© 1989 by NTC Publishing Group, 4255 West Touhy Avenue,
Lincolnwood (Chicago), Illinois 60646-1975 U.S.A.
Manufactured in the United States of America.
Library of Congress Catalog Card Number: 88-62055

1 2 3 4 5 6 7 8 9 TS 9 8 7 6 5 4 3

To the Student

Have you ever been on a safari? A safari is a hunting expedition, usually in Africa. If you are on a safari, you would like to discover something. People on a traditional safari would like to discover where a wild animal — maybe a lion — is.

Discovery is what *Safari Grammar* is all about. But *Safari Grammar* will help you discover something much different than African animals. *Safari Grammar* will lead you on a journey into the English language. (Certainly less dangerous than lions, and tigers, and bears, but just as exciting!)

You will discover parts of speech, the jobs specific kinds of words do, and how to use words correctly. *Safari Grammar* will also give you the opportunity to practice what you discover through exercises and written activities.

By the way, safaris usually have guides — experts who "know the way" and can instruct and advise. *Safari Grammar* has guides also, and they are guaranteed to make your journey pleasant and rewarding. These guides will help you understand the basic rules of grammar. The more you understand, the more you will be able to discover on your own. So relax, meet your guides and enjoy the journey.

Foreword

Jungle Jack and his entourage of creatures —
alligators, frogs, storks, snakes, rabbits, moles,
birds — may not be typical guides through
English grammar, but in this original book they
prove themselves to be informative, entertaining
companions as they explain the characteristics of
nouns, pronouns, determiners, adjectives, verbs,
contractions, adverbs and other parts of speech.

Safari Grammar leads students cheerfully
through the essentials of English grammar. Its
delightful illustrations serve as functional teaching
aids that reinforce grammar points. These stimu-
lating cartoons will engage the students' interest
and make them feel that English grammar can
be fun.

Safari Grammar is intended for all students of

English as an enjoyable, unique way to journey through the basics of English grammar. Students of English will thoroughly enjoy this refreshing introduction to grammar. Native speakers will find this book an entertaining way to brush up on their verb tenses, to reacquaint themselves with the main parts of speech, or to review grammatical structures. *Safari Grammar* provides the teacher and student with a delightful initial overview of grammar. Teachers may wish to use the text as a launching point for more in-depth studies.

The book follows the same pattern of organization throughout. A rule is introduced and explained through an entertaining dialogue between the creatures. Examples are given. Rules are then set off from the text for high visual impact. An exercise, to be done on separate paper, is provided for each grammar point introduced. Grammar points are recycled throughout the text, and incorporated into subsequent lessons.

The creatures speak in a natural, realistic manner (for creatures that is!). In addition, the occasional idiomatic expression or unusual vocabulary item is highlighted and explained. An index of grammar points is included for easy reference.

For beginners, *Safari Grammar* provides the ideal way to stimulate the students' curiosity while introducing them to grammar basics. For other students, *Safari Grammar* can be used as an eye-opener — a book with real personality that will reacquaint students with grammar through clearly illustrated rules.

Contents

A **noun** is either a

person, a **place,** or a **thing.**

A **person** is a human like yourself—also teacher, boss, friend, mother, father, etc. Actually everyone in the whole world is a person, or noun.

A **place** can be anywhere you go. It can be an amusement park, classroom, bathroom, closet, city, town, clubhouse, jail, hothouse, nursery, etc. **Can you think of any other place?**

A **thing** can be any object: a cup, finger, lamp, car, airplane, swimming pool, television set, computer, tree house, or any kind of furniture. Look around your room. I'll bet you can pick out at least ten things right away.

3

either a **person,** **place, thing,** or creature!

EXERCISE 1

There are two nouns in each sentence. List numbers 1 to 8 in the left margin on a separate piece of paper. List the two nouns in each sentence. Example: 1. boy, store.

1. The boy ran to the store.
2. The lady mended the skirt.
3. The cat ate its dinner.
4. The dog buried its bone.
5. That cat caught a fish.
6. This rabbit has whiskers.
7. The desk is in the classroom.
8. The frog lived in the pond.

6

Proper nouns differ from other nouns (common nouns) because proper nouns are **specific** persons, places, things, and creatures, like **King Kong, John, Mary, New York, London**...

This is a fast exercise.

EXERCISE 2

Take a separate piece of paper and divide it into four columns as shown below. List three proper nouns under each heading.

Person	Place	Thing	Creature
	New York		

Here is an example of a **proper noun** (specific noun). There are several kangaroos (common nouns), but there is only one Matilda (proper noun—because she is a *specific* kangaroo).

Here comes Matilda!

kangaroos
(common noun)

Matilda (proper noun)

12

EXERCISE 3

Each sentence below contains a common and a proper noun. Please list them on a separate piece of paper. Example: 1. teacher (common noun), Central School (proper noun)

1. The teacher taught at Central School.
2. The student called to John.
3. San Francisco is a city.
4. Mr. Smith went to the bakery.
5. Macy's is a large store.
6. Dr. Jones helped the child.
7. Rover had spots.
8. Laura ate the pie.
9. The house belongs to the Smiths.
10. Sunday is a holiday.

Oops! Almost forgot... besides real nouns, there are also **imaginary nouns.**

Are you REAL?

Some **imaginary nouns** are fictitious characters in storybooks and movies (like Rocky, Mickey Mouse, Superman, or Don Quixote) and imaginary places (like the Land of Oz or Gotham).

So far we've learned that a noun is either a person, a place, a thing, or a creature—and that they can be real or imaginary.

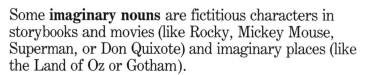

15

*Another way of saying ''We've finished studying all the nouns.''

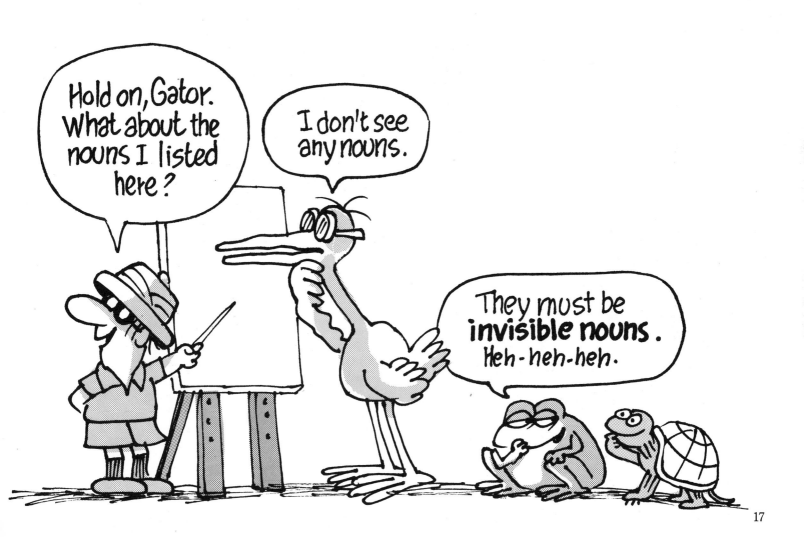

17

Right you are, Frog! We are INVISIBLE NOUNS.*

Not all things can be seen. They are truly there—sometimes in your mind. A thought, an idea, a dream, hope, health, and happiness. They are called **invisible nouns.** Others can be heard, like a scream, a moan, a groan, a cry, a whimper, a shriek, a sob, or a burp. And there are other invisible nouns that can be felt, like fear, sorrow, hunger, or hurt. Or they can be something like democracy, freedom, or peace.

18

*Also known as **abstract nouns.**

Can't you keep your **invisible nouns** quiet?

WOOoo

WAAAAA

EXERCISE 5

On a separate piece of paper, write down the invisible noun in each sentence.

Example: 1. thirst.

1. John was dying of thirst.
2. The mummy let out a blood-curdling scream.
3. The frightened puppy made a little whimper.
4. Mary glowed with happiness.
5. The wolf's howl could be heard for miles.

singular   plural

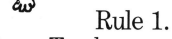

Up here!

Rule 1.
To change most nouns from singular to plural, add **s** to the end of the noun.

Singular	**Plural**
boy	boys
cow	cows
apple	apples

And that's **plural** too: many kangaroos.

EXERCISE 6

The list below has both singular and plural nouns. On a separate piece of paper, list *only* the plural nouns.
Example: books

boys   dinosaurs   car   dog   rabbit

John   man   boy   bats

Mary   candies   apple   candy   books

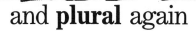

and **plural** again

However, adding **-s** doesn't always make nouns plural.

Here are some more rules for making nouns plural.

Rule 2.
Add **-es** to nouns ending in **ch, sh, s, x,** and **z.**

Singular	Plural
beach	beach**es**
bush	bush**es**
box	box**es**
bus	bus**es**
buzz	buzz**es**

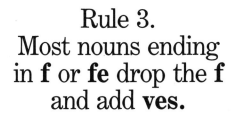

Rule 3.
Most nouns ending in **f** or **fe** drop the **f** and add **ves.**

Singular	Plural
loaf	loa**ves**
leaf	lea**ves**
hoof	hoo**ves**
shelf	shel**ves**
wife	wi**ves**

Rule 4.
Add **s** to nouns that have a **vowel** before their **y** ending.

Singular	Plural
boy	boy**s**
monkey	monkey**s**

There's more over here.

*All the letters in the alphabet are consonants except the **bold letters,** which are vowels:

EXERCISE 7

On a separate piece of paper, copy the following nouns and write their plural forms.

Rule 2. wish, fox, pass, ash, stitch, patch, class
Rule 3. leaf, hoof, wolf, knife
Rule 4. alley, journey, valley, tray, key, turkey, play
Rule 5. story, mystery, city, holly, jelly

In rules 4 and 5, underline the letter before the final **y** to show why you have made the plural in that way.

Plural nouns are easy.

Especially for rabbits.

27

Possessive nouns show ownership by

Rule 1.
Add **-'s** to a singular noun to make it possessive.

Noun	Possessive Noun
frog	frog's chair
alligator	alligator's shoes
Jack	Jack's car
Mr. Davis	Mr. Davis's car
Ms. Foss	Ms. Foss's eggs

adding -'s or just -'

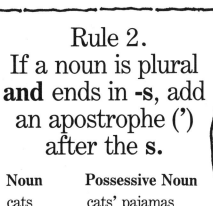

Like when there is more than one cat... **The cats' pajamas.**

But plural nouns that **don't end in -s** also follow rule 1: the **mice's tails.**

29

EXERCISE 8

On a separate piece of paper, copy the following words and write their possessive forms.

cow, horse, friend, dress, Dr. Jones, boys, classes, men, women, child, children, sheep, basket, gorilla, lamps, chair, chairs, card, flowers, countries

Give me an example of a possessive noun.

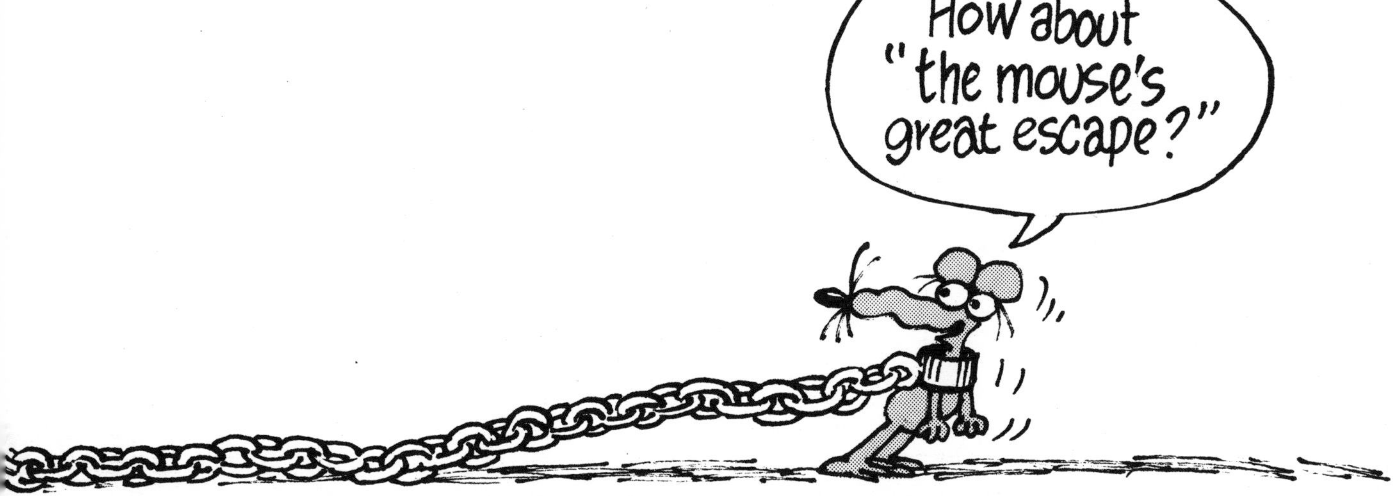
How about "the mouse's great escape?"

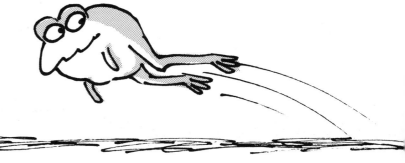

33

Pronouns take the place of nouns.

Subject	I	you	he	she	it	we	they
Object	me	you	him	her	it	us	them

36

Examples:

I gave **it** to **them.**
We know **her** and **him.**
They will follow **you.**
She studied with **him.**

EXERCISE 9

On a separate piece of paper, number from 1 to 10.
Write the pronoun or pronouns that match the
given noun.

Noun	Pronoun(s)		
1. child	he	she	them
2. Mr. Rogers	he	she	us
3. pizza	you	us	it
4. Disneyland	us	I	it
5. aunt	you	them	she
6. potatoes	they	them	you
7. mirror	us	him	it
8. newspaper	me	they	it
9. poppies	they	them	us
10. library	me	us	it

Are **you** a personal pronoun?

Of course **I** am!

38

Adjectives:	my	your		her		our	their
			his		its		
Pronouns:	mine	yours		hers		ours	theirs
			his				

Examples:

Adjective	Pronoun
It is **her** book.	The book is **hers**.
It is **his** book.	The book is **his**.
It is **my** book.	The book is **mine**.

40

41

43

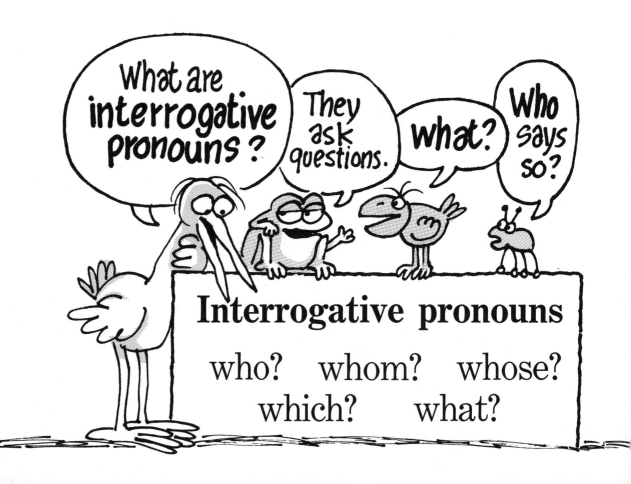

It's exercise time.

Example:

Whose dog is this?
What is happening?

EXERCISE 11

On a separate piece of paper, number from 1 to 5. Write the missing interrogative pronoun.

Example: 1.___Who___ knocked over the chair?

1. _____ lives here?
2. _____ is your name?
3. To _____ do we owe this honor?
4. _____ book is this?
5. _____ one of you ate all the candy?

45

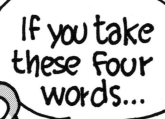

If you take these four words...

...you can make these 12 **indefinite pronouns**.

any =	any**one**	any**body**	any**thing**
every =	every**one**	every**body**	every**thing**
no =	no **one**	no**body**	no**thing**
some =	some**one**	some**body**	some**thing**

46

47

Reflexive pronouns end in **self** (singular) or **selves** (plural).
They always have a noun or pronoun that they refer to.

I taught them to **myself.**

Singular

I and me = myself
you = yourself
he = himself
she = herself
it = itself

Plural

our = ourselves
you = yourselves
they = themselves

Example: I bought myself a sweater.

I exercise myself.

EXERCISE 13

Take a separate piece of paper and number from 1 to 9. Fill in the missing **self** or **selves** pronoun.

Example: I poured ___myself___ some lemonade.

1. I saw _____ in the mirror
2. Why did you write _____ a letter?
3. Clothes don't wash_____.
4. She taught it to_____.
5. Ted splashed paint on_____.
6. Both of you took photos of_____?
7. He sang_____ a lullaby.
8. Snakes move_____ by wiggling.

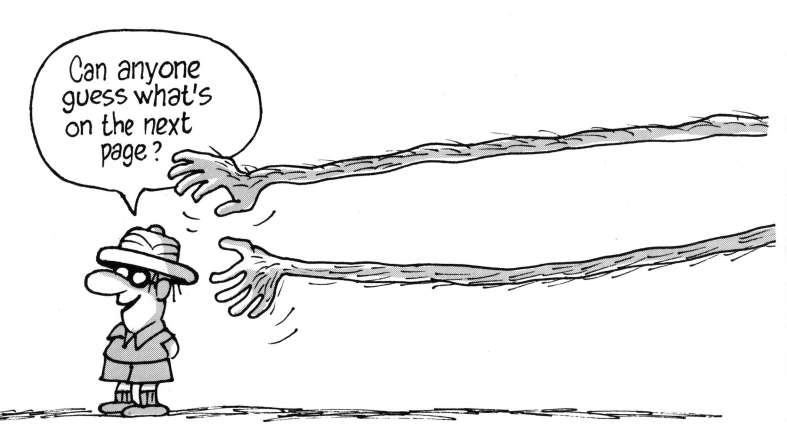

51

Noun Huggers*

Find a noun hugger and you'll find a noun. Here
are some noun huggers that are often used:

a	every	that
an	many	this
the	some	these
		those

Possessive adjectives are also noun huggers
(my, his, her, its, our, your, their).
Remember there is **always** a noun following
a hugger.

a cowboy

52

*Noun huggers are also known as **determiners**.

an elephant

the rabbit

But before we practice **huggers**, we must learn these two, simple rules.

The Use of **a** and **an**

Rule 1. If a noun begins with a vowel (a, e, i, o, u), use the hugger **an**.

Example: **a** elephant (wrong)
an elephant (right)

Rule 2. If a noun begins with a consonant, use the hugger **a**.

Example: **a** cow

*As shown on page 24, all the letters in the alphabet are consonants except these **bold letters**, whic

EXERCISE 14

On a separate piece of paper, copy these sentences and underline the huggers. There is more than one hugger in some of these sentences.

Example: 1. <u>An</u> elephant is <u>a</u> huge animal.

1. An elephant is a huge animal.
2. The firefighter put out our fire.
3. My snake eats mice.
4. Your car is in my way.
5. His books and her skates were on the shelf.
6. The rabbit lost its carrot.
7. This book is funny.
8. An apple and a sandwich are good for lunch.
9. A girl opened an umbrella.
10. An aardvark is an interesting animal.

Don't forget to do your hugger exercise.

are vowels: **a** b c d **e** f g h **i** j k l m n **o** p q r s t **u** v w x y z

Adjectives describe nouns and pronouns.

Can you name the adjectives?

58

When comparing people or things , add **-er** or **-est*** on the end of the adjective.

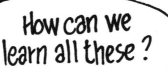

How can we learn all these?

Maybe we can sing them?

However the -er and -est endings don't work with **irregular adjectives.**

Irregular Adjectives

good well	better	best
bad	worse	worst
much many	more	most

61

* A "rap song" is talking in rhythm, sometimes with rhyme.

Adjectives usually appear before the nouns they describe.
Examples: The **fat** cat. The **bald** man. The **happy** child.

Sometimes more than one adjective is used to describe a noun.
Example: The **little red** ball went over the fence.

And did you know numbers were adjectives?
Example: **Fifteen** camels (describes how many camels)

Did you notice? At the top of this page we said adjectives usually appear before the nouns they describe. On these pages were some examples in which adjectives follow the words they describe.

The fox is **handsome.**

The turtle is
tired.

EXERCISE 15

Take a separate piece of paper and
recopy the sentences below. Underline all
the **adjectives** that describe nouns or
pronouns.

Example: 1. The teacher is __intelligent__.

1. The tough team won the game.
2. His mule is lazy.
3. The ugly crime was mysterious.
4. My purple cow gave white milk.
5. This fine student is very bright.
6. Eight girls went to see the circus.
7. Your itchy dog has fleas.
8. The muddy swamp is deep and cold.
9. The hot, bright sun was welcome.

This is
a **light**
exercise.

Verbs show action.

Verbs tell what nouns and pronouns do.
Example: Everyone **ran** from the spears and
arrows.
The verb **ran** shows action.

The verb shows what the noun **does.**

Example: The turtle **sleeps** on the rock everyday.
The verb shows what he **does** (sleeps).

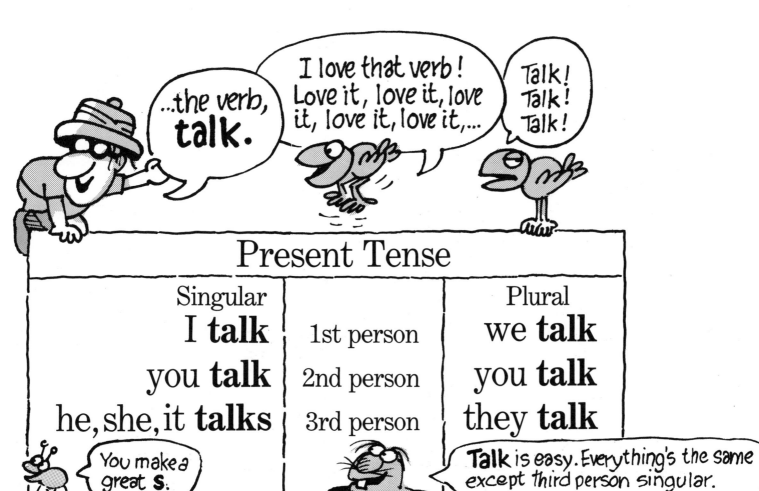

Present Tense

Singular		Plural
I **talk**	1st person	we **talk**
you **talk**	2nd person	you **talk**
he, she, it **talks**	3rd person	they **talk**

*The **s** ending is called an inflection.

71

When the noun or pronoun is third person singular, always add an **s** ending to the verb.

← **Here**
(third person singular)

But not
(third person

John talk**s**.   Mary talk**s**.   The parrot talk**s**.

here ➡

plural)

John, Mary, and the parrot talk. (They talk.)

Add **s** here

he, she, it
John, Mary,   } **talks**
the parrot

But, don't add **s**
on the others.

I, you, we, they
John *and* Mary   } **talk**
the parrots

EXERCISE 16

Write three sentences using the
verb **run** and three sentences
using the verb **runs**.

Tenses, present and past

Tenses show the **time** of the action. For example, **present tense** shows action that is not completed. **Past tense** shows action that is completed. Here are some examples using the verb **mail.**

Present tense
(The action is not completed — this action happens again and again.)

Past tense
(The action is completed.)

75

*I, you, he, she, it, we, they

78

be

Past Tense

Singular	Plural
I ⎱ **was**	we ⎱
you ⎰ **were**	you ⎰ **were**
he, she, it ⎱ **was**	they ⎰

That's simple. Past tense is either **was** or **were**.

EXERCISE 18

On a separate piece of paper, make up sentences using each of the seven pronouns with the present and past tenses of the verb **be**. After writing each sentence, say it aloud.

79

Present Tense			
Singular		**Plural**	
I, you **do**		we, you, they **do**	
he, she, it **does**			

Past Tense			
Singular		**Plural**	
I, you **did**		we, you, they **did**	
he, she, it			

EXERCISE 20

Make up sentences using each of the seven pronouns (see page 81) with the present and past tenses of the verb **do.** Say each sentence aloud after writing it. 83

*A common error when using the third person singular. He **do.** (wrong) He **does.** (right)

We've already studied present and past tenses. And we've studied three important verbs (**be, do, have**). These verbs are also used as auxiliary* verbs and will help us with the four new tenses we are about to learn.

But first let's review present and past tenses that we studied on page 74.

Present: The action is not finished. It happens again and again.

*Auxiliary verbs are often called helping verbs. They are used with other verbs.

Past: The action is finished.

85

Future Tense

(The action did not begin yet.)

Simple. Use either **shall** or **will** with the verb.

Future Tense

I
you
he, she, it
we
you
they

} **shall mail**
or
will mail

EXERCISE 21

Make up sentences using each of the seven pronouns with the future tense of the verb **talk.** Say each sentence aloud after writing it. Example: I **will talk** to her.

Time to exercise.

The **Present Progressive** is used to report

Compare with present tense on page 74.

I am mailing the letter.

(Present Progressive:
Is happening now and will
probably be completed soon.)

present events.

Present Progressive uses auxiliary verbs like **be, have,** and **do**... but Present tense doesn't.

And it has an **-ing** ending (mail**ing**).

Present Progressive

I **am**
you **are**
he, she, it **is**
we **are**
you **are**
they **are**
} mailing

EXERCISE 22

Make up sentences using each of the seven pronouns* with the present progressive tense of the verb **help.** Then do the same with the present tense of the verb **help.** Use **now** in the present progressive sentences and **everyday** in the present sentences. Say each sentence aloud after writing it. Examples: I **am helping** them now. (present progressive) I **help** them everyday. (present)

*I, you, he, she, it, we, they

Past Progressive

Compare how the past progressive differs from the past tense.

━━━━ Past Tense ━━━━

━━━━ Past

(The action is completed.)

(A past event that

And like Present Progressive it uses auxiliary verbs (was, were) and ends in **-ing**.

Progressive ▬▬▬

...when I was unexpectedly detained.

MEN AT WORK

hasn't been completed.)

Past Progressive

I	**was**	
you	**were**	
he, she, it	**was**	
we	**were**	} mailing
you	**were**	
they	**were**	

EXERCISE 23

Make up sentences using each of the seven pronouns* with the past progressive tense of the verb **earn.** Then do the same with the past tense of the verb **earn.** Use **before** or **when** in the past progressive sentences, use **yesterday** or **last week** in the past sentences. Say each sentence aloud after writing it. Examples: I **was earning** a dollar a day before my promotion. (past progressive)
I **earned** a dollar yesterday. (past)

*I, you, he, she, it, we, they   93

The **Present Perfect** is used to talk about

The action begins in the past
and continues to the present.

94

a **past** event that relates to the **present**.

Present Perfect

I **have**
you **have**
he, she, it **has** } **mailed**
we **have**
you **have**
they **have**

After you.

EXERCISE 24

Make up sentences using each of the seven pronouns* with the present perfect tense of the verb **watch**. Then do the same with the past and past progressive tenses of the verb **watch**. Say each sentence aloud after writing it.

Examples: I **watched** the parade. (past)
I **have watched** this parade ever since** I was a child. (present perfect)
I **was watching** the parade when it began to rain. (past progressive)

*I, you, he, she, it, we, they
for and **since** are often used in present perfect sentences.

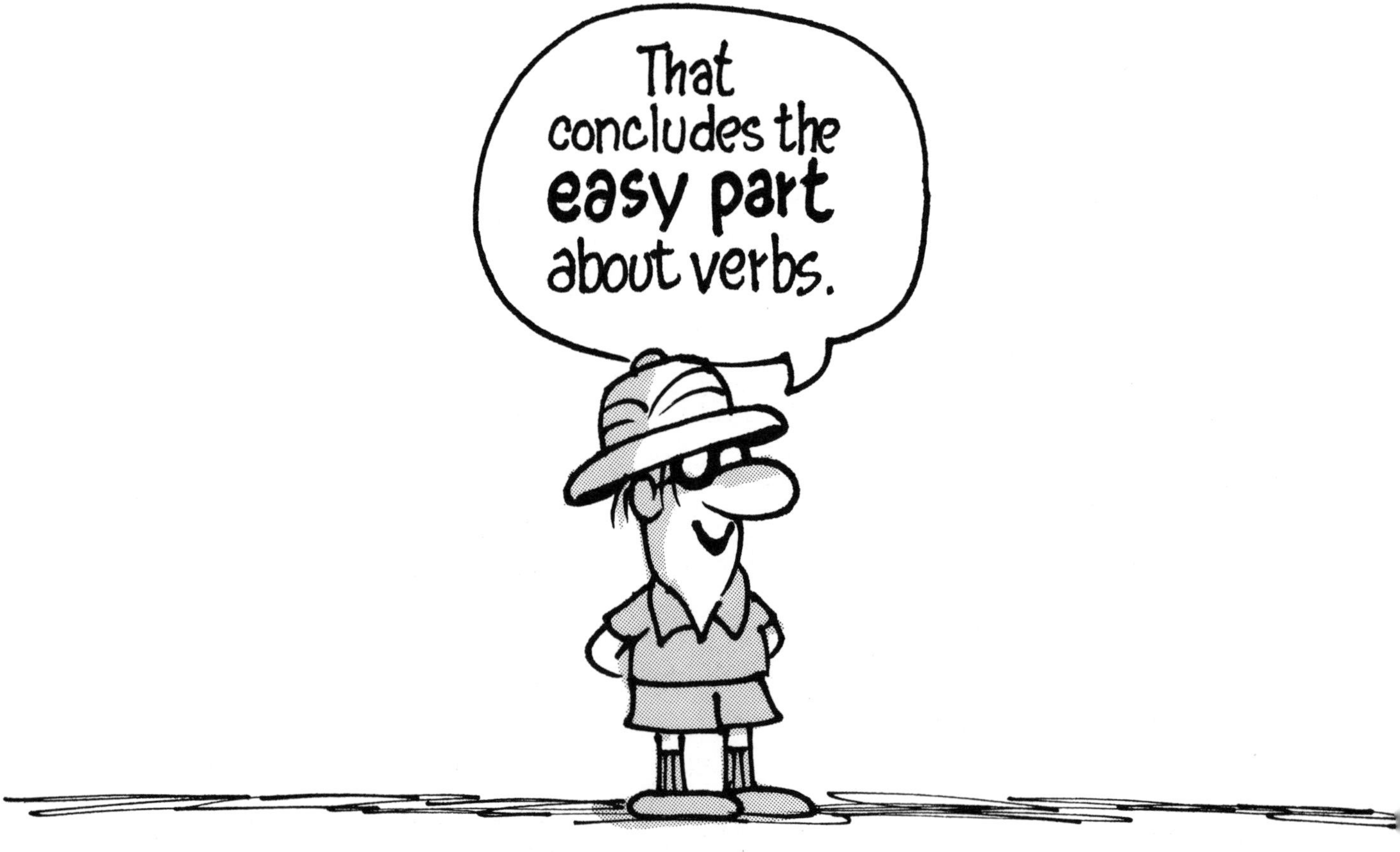
That concludes the **easy part** about verbs.

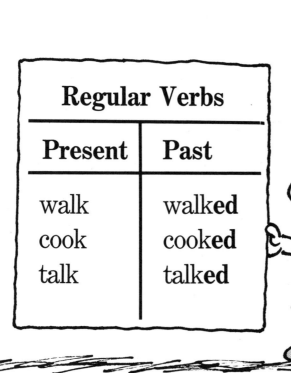

We all know that adding **-ed** or **-d** changes a verb from present to past tense.

Irregular Verbs

Present	Past	Past Participle *
awake	awoke	awaked, awoken
be	was, were	been
beat	beat	beat
become	became	become
begin	began	begun
bite	bit	bitten
bleed	bled	bled
blow	blew	blown
break	broke	broken
bring	brought	brought
build	built	built
buy	bought	bought
catch	caught	caught
choose	chose	chosen
come	came	come
cut	cut	cut
do	did	done
draw	drew	drawn
drink	drank	drunk
drive	drove	driven
eat	ate	eaten
fall	fell	fallen
feed	fed	fed
feel	felt	felt
fight	fought	fought
find	found	found
fly	flew	flown
forget	forgot	forgotten
freeze	froze	frozen
get	got	gotten

*Used with auxiliary verbs to form the
present perfect tense. (See pages 94 and 95.)

Present	Past	Past Participle [*]	Present	Past	Past Participle [*]
give	gave	given	see	saw	seen
go	went	gone	sell	sold	sold
grow	grew	grown	send	sent	sent
have	had	had	set	set	set
hear	heard	heard	shake	shook	shaken
hide	hid	hidden	shine	shone	shone
hit	hit	hit	show	showed	shown, showed
hold	held	held	shut	shut	shut
hurt	hurt	hurt	sing	sang	sung
keep	kept	kept	sit	sat	sat
know	knew	known	sleep	slept	slept
lay[1]	laid	laid	speak	spoke	spoken
leave	left	left	speed	sped	sped
lend	lent	lent	spend	spent	spent
let	let	let	stand	stood	stood
lie[2]	lay	lain	steal	stole	stolen
lose[3]	lost	lost	swear	swore	sworn
make	made	made	swim	swam	swum
mean	meant	meant	take	took	taken
meet	met	met	teach	taught	taught
pay	paid	paid	tear	tore	torn
put	put	put	tell	told	told
quit	quit	quit	think	thought	thought
read	read[4]	read	throw	threw	thrown
ride	rode	ridden	understand	understood	understood
ring	rang	rung	wake	woke, waked	waked
rise	rose	risen	wear	wore	worn
run	ran	run	win	won	won
say	said	said	write	wrote	written

1. It is irregular in spelling only.
2. There is also a regular verb **lie,** with a different meaning. Check your dictionary.
3. Do not confuse **lose** with the regular verb **loose.** Check your dictionary.
4. Note the different pronunciation. **Read** present tense rhymes with **deed. Read** past tense and past participle rhyme with **head.**

103

105

OK, the party's over. It's exercise time!

EXERCISE 25

On a separate piece of paper, write the present, past, and past participle of the first ten irregular verbs (page 100). Write each one five times and practice saying it aloud.

Tomorrow do the same thing with the next ten. Continue doing this each day until you've finished the entire list of irregular verbs. Perhaps you might even want to repeat the entire lesson?

Maybe you would like to try rap songs. Here are some rhyme groups: blow, fly, grow, know, throw— tear, wear—lend, send, spend— bleed, feed, meet, read—break, speak— bring, buy, catch, fight, teach, think— choose, freeze—drink, ring, sing, swim—lay, pay

Right you are, Gator. **It's** contraction time.

Contractions are shortened forms of two words.

Example: **Let us** do it. **Let's** do it.

Note: the letter **u** of **us** is replaced by an apostrophe (').

Examples with **not:***

cannot	=	can't
could not	=	couldn't
will not	=	won't
would not	=	wouldn't
do not	=	don't
does not	=	doesn't

*Note: The apostrophe takes the place of **o** in **not**.

*Frog is agreeing with Gator because **what's** *is* a contraction.

109

be

Don't forget these three.

I	**am**		I'm
he			he's
she	**is**		she's
it			it's
we			we're
you	**are**		you're
they			they're

Example: **I'm** busy.

have

I			I've
we	**have**		we've
you	(+ verb)		you've
they			they've
he			he's
she	**has**		she's
it	(+ verb)		it's

Example: **He's** paid the bill.

shall or will

I			I'll
he			he'll
she	**shall**		she'll
it	or		it'll
we	**will**		we'll
you			you'll
they			they'll

Example: **It'll** be here soon.

what's   where's   who's

would

I					I'd
he					he'd
she			would		she'd
we					we'd
you					you'd
they					they'd

Example: **She'd** eat if she could.

EXERCISE 26

On a separate piece of paper, write the contractions where possible in the following sentences. Example:
1. They've bought three cars.

1. They have bought three cars.
2. He cannot find the street.
3. What is his name?
4. Let us be friends.
5. They will be here tomorrow.
6. He would like to join our club.
7. You do not deserve to win.
8. I am going to New York.

Adverbs tell either **when, where,** or **how.**

Adverbs are like adjectives because they **describe**. Adjectives describe nouns and **adverbs describe verbs.**

He ate **early.**
(when)

He lives **here.**
(where)

She spoke **softly.**
(how)

113

Adding **-er** and **-est**

Jungle Jack
runs **fast.**

Gator runs
faster.

Stork runs **fastest.**

These endings are called adverb inflections.

adding **-ly** to an adjective.

EXERCISE 27

Fill in the blanks on a separate piece of paper.

Adjectives	Adverbs
1. The quick boy	He ran ___quickly___ .
2. The patient man	He waited _____ .
3. The quiet evening	We spent the evening _____ .
4. The loud car	The car banged _____ .
5. The sweet child	The child smiled _____ .

Ready for what's next?

119

Index

Ancona Graphics typography
San Mateo, California